I0533329

I Am Ashley

*A True Story of Growing Up Trans in a World
That Said I Couldn't Be Her*

Written by Ashley J. Webb

Published by **Ashley J. Webb**
Printed in the United States of America.

Table of Contents

Dedication

To Eve and Alyssa —

You didn't know me, but you helped save me.

In the chaos that followed my nodule diagnosis, your voices grounded me.

Chewed Gum gave me focus, clarity, and something to hold onto when I was ready to give up.

This book is my truth. But the spark that lit it?

That came from you.

Thank you — for helping me survive long enough to finish it.

And for reminding me I wasn't alone.

Ashley

What Lit the Spark

This Book Exists Because...

Because *Ice Princess* from **Walt Disney Pictures** made me cry — not just because of the skating, but because I saw a girl chasing her truth and being told it wasn't enough.

Because **Rachel Platten's** *Fight Song* wasn't just music — it was a reminder that even when your voice shakes, it still counts.

Because someone, somewhere, needed to read the story I never had growing up.

This book exists because I refused to disappear.

Introduction

This is not a story built on slogans.

This is not a manifesto, a trend, or a movement.

This is my life.

> *"No, being trans is not some fad.*
> *Here's what it cost me to be honest."*
> *"No, identity isn't something adults*
> *should push onto children. Here's what*
> *it looks like when you figure it out the*
> *hard way — with pain, time, and truth."*

I didn't become Ashley because someone told me to.

I didn't transition for attention, or because of social

media, or because of some political agenda.
I did it because I had no other choice — because
being anything else was killing me slowly.

This book isn't here to convince you what to
believe.
It's here to show you what it feels like to grow up
feminine in a world that punishes it,
to live in a body that confuses everyone,
and to fight every day for the right to simply be.

If you're trans, I hope this book feels like
someone finally sees you.
If you're not, I hope it helps you understand — and
protect — the ones who are still figuring it out.

This is my story. But it belongs to anyone who's
ever been told they don't get to exist.

The snow was soft, silent, glowing under the stars. I pressed my hand to the window, watching it fall. The world looked peaceful out there. Clean. Honest.

I whispered, "I wish I could be a real girl."

I didn't know the truth yet. I didn't know she already existed — buried under misunderstanding, silence, and medical mystery.

But in that moment, all I felt was the ache of a wish I didn't know had always been mine.

I was born into the world with no say in who I'd be.

The delivery room was warm and bright, the kind of place where people make big declarations with absolute certainty — like what a baby is. "It's a boy," they said. Three little words that would shape everything about how I was raised, treated, and even punished.

My name had already been decided months earlier, etched into baby shower cards and ultrasound photos — James.

But nobody stopped to ask what *I* felt. Nobody paused to notice that the body they saw and the soul I carried were not on the same page.

No one knew the storm that would one day come from assigning me that name. James. A name that fit like a costume two sizes too big. A name I would carry like a weight until the day I realized it never belonged to me.

My parents were both hard workers, just trying to make their way in a difficult world.

They weren't cruel. They weren't monsters. They were simply doing what they thought was right — raising a child the way they had been raised, with rules, expectations, and survival as the goal. Life wasn't soft for them, so they didn't know how to make it soft for me.

My dad worked long hours and came home tired. Then my mom would leave for her shift, often after holding everything else together all day — the meals, the laundry, the scraped knees. It was like a passing of the baton in a never-ending relay, with no rest for either of them.

They did their best with what they had, but emotions were luxuries we didn't always have space for. Tenderness was something you earned, not something you received just for existing.

And so, when I started showing signs of softness — when I moved differently, reacted emotionally, or didn't match what they imagined a "boy" should be — they didn't panic. They didn't overreact. They probably just thought it was normal. Maybe part of growing up. They were first-time parents, after all.

What they didn't know was that I was already breaking — quietly, invisibly — trying to be someone I wasn't just to make them proud.

We lived in a major city — not some tiny town, but a place big enough to get lost in. Still, family was everywhere.

My dad's mother and siblings were in the city with us, never too far away. Some of my mom's family lived in the surrounding areas, and even a few right there in the city too. It wasn't just my parents watching me grow up — it was cousins, aunts, uncles, and grandparents. There were eyes everywhere. Expectations came from all directions, not just the roof over our heads.

Back then, gender roles were followed the way people followed traffic lights — without question. Boys did one thing, girls did another, and anyone who didn't fit neatly into those boxes was seen as broken. Not different. **Broken.** It wasn't about curiosity or individuality. It was about normalcy, and survival. You followed the script or you got cast out.

You have to remember, this was the 1980s. Gay and lesbian individuals were being targeted in many of the same ways trans people are today.

Discrimination wasn't hidden — it was public, loud, and often deadly. Being different in any visible way was dangerous. And in a family where conformity meant safety, there wasn't room for questioning what you were told to be.

I don't remember everything from that time clearly — memories from early childhood can blur like old photographs left out in the sun. But I've seen the photos. The birthday parties were all themed the same: trucks, action heroes, camouflage, sports. The kinds of things boys were supposed to like. The cake colors were bold. The wrapping paper was blue. No one meant harm by it. They were just following what society told them a "boy's party" should look like.

And so was I — smiling in the pictures, opening gifts I was supposed to be excited about. No one could see what wasn't there. No one noticed what was missing.

But you can only hide from yourself for so long.

Chapter 2: A Spreading Crack in the Windshield

By the time I hit first grade, the world had started drawing lines — not with words, but with expectations.

I don't remember a lot from those early school years, but I do remember the birthday parties. They were always loud and full of energy, packed with little boys hyped up on cake and plastic weapons. Mine were no different. The themes were always something like Ninja Turtles, Power Rangers, or camouflage — the kind of stuff boys were supposed to like. The kind of stuff that told everyone I was exactly who they thought I was.

I smiled in the pictures, ripped open the wrapping paper, posed with the action figures. It was easy to play along. Easy to be what everyone already believed I was. But something about it never felt personal. The joy felt borrowed — like I was celebrating someone else's birthday, in someone else's skin.

At recess, the divide between boys and girls had already begun, even if no one talked about it yet. The boys ran wild — chasing each other, wrestling, throwing things. I joined in when I had to. I could laugh and keep up. But more often than not, I mostly stayed to myself. I loved it when it had just rained before recess. The playground was built on a hill, and the runoff would trickle down in little streams. I'd crouch in the mud and build dams with my hands, trying to hold the water back. It was quiet there — peaceful in a way nothing else was.

The school had a zip line at the time, and I remember the day it had to be taken down. I fell off it — hard. And that was the first time I started to notice something no one else had said out loud: my muscles didn't seem to work like the other boys'. Not quite. I wasn't as strong or fast or sure-footed. It wasn't just about feeling different on the inside anymore. My body had started to confirm it.

In the classroom, things were quieter. I liked art time and story hour, when everything slowed down and softened. No one was pushing or shouting. We sat in rows or at tables, gluing shapes to paper or listening to books being read aloud. I didn't stand out, and I didn't want to. But there were tiny flickers — moments when I noticed that the kids who were praised for being gentle or imaginative were usually the girls.

I didn't have the words for it then, but it stung a little. Like I was being told that the parts of me I liked best didn't belong to me.

Sometimes, when the teacher asked what a book was about, I wouldn't retell the actual story — I'd make one up based on the pictures. Whole new adventures. My own version of what should have happened. The teachers never seemed to mind. They'd smile, nod, and give me a star to add to my Book-It badge. I was proud of those stars. A few more, and I could redeem them for a free pizza. That sticker meant more than food. It meant I had done something right.

And then there was Halloween.

That year, I went as a witch. My mom had dressed as a witch for her job, and I wanted to match her.

Maybe it was the hat, or the long flowing fabric, or maybe just the chance to be something a little magical. The costume swished when I walked. It felt like something out of a fairy tale. At one of the houses, a woman handing out candy smiled and said to my mom, "What a beautiful daughter. Nice costume."

My mom didn't correct her.

That moment stayed with me — not because it embarrassed me, but because for the first time, someone looked at me and saw something that made sense.

Looking back now, I can see how the crack in the windshield kept spreading — quietly, invisibly — through moments no one else noticed. But one of the first times I felt it truly break was at home, not school. I was just a kid, still learning how the world worked. I sat down to pee — not because I thought anything of it, but because it felt normal. Comfortable.

But my dad saw me. And in a flash, it wasn't about comfort. It was about shame.

I didn't have the words for it then, but that moment taught me something loud and clear: even the way I used the bathroom could get me in trouble. Even my body's comfort came with conditions.

And a crack became a fracture.

Chapter 3: He Belongs to Her

Middle school wasn't like the movies — no lockers clanging or crowded hallways full of drama. Not where I lived. I was still in that rural town, still at a school where we had recess and a playground, even as our bodies started changing and the world started tightening its grip on us.

I wasn't thinking much about my body back then. Not in the way they wanted me to. But my body had already started changing — forming breasts like all the other girls. It wasn't something I asked for. It just happened. Quietly. Naturally. No one around me seemed to notice — or if they did, they just chalked it up to me being fat.

I didn't have the words for any of it. Not dysphoria, not identity. I didn't even have the words to ask why it was happening. I just knew I was supposed to pretend it wasn't.

So I did what I always did — tried to get through the day without causing a stir.

It was warm out — the kind of heat that made even the teachers move slower. I wore a tank top. Not to make a statement. Not to stand out. Just because it was hot and it felt good to let my skin breathe. Nothing about it seemed like a big deal.

But someone noticed.

It was a boy. I still remember his face, the way his voice cut through the noise around us. *"Ew, that's gross,"* he said, pointing directly at my armpit hair. Loud enough for other kids to hear. Loud enough to make sure I felt it.

Then he escalated. Called a teacher over. Still pointing, still acting like I was something shameful just for existing in the body I had. *"That's gross,"* he repeated. Not even trying to hide it.

No one asked how I felt. No one asked why I had hair there or what it meant to me. The teacher just looked at me, looked at my body, and decided it was inappropriate — not because of what I was wearing, but because of what my body had become.

After class, that same teacher pulled me aside. Calm voice, like she was doing me a favor. She told me I wasn't allowed to wear tank tops to school anymore. No real explanation. No rule book. Just… don't.

I remember walking out at the end of the day, seeing other girls in tank tops — straps thinner than mine, shirts shorter than mine. No one was pulling them aside. No one was telling them their bodies were wrong.

And that's when it really sank in: **this wasn't about clothing. It was about me.**
I wasn't being treated fairly — and maybe I never would be.

The following school year, everything started changing — for him, too.

The same boy who had pointed at my armpit hair and called me "gross" had finally hit puberty. I remember it vividly, not because of him, but because of how much worse it made everything feel. He wasn't teasing anymore — he was talking like he owned the world. Like the girls around us were there for his commentary.

He'd say things like, *"Have you seen hers? Her areolas are getting huge."* Loud. Cruel. Like it was funny. Like girls were just parts he could rate and measure.

It made me sick.

Not just because it was disgusting — it was — but because I was going through some of the same changes. My areolas were changing too.

My body was still doing what it had always done: ignoring the script and moving in its own direction.

All I could think was, *I hope I never become like him.*
I didn't know who I was yet. But I knew, without question, **who I wasn't**.

Had I been raised as a girl, I probably would've been told during puberty that girls shave their armpits. It would've come up casually, like a rule everyone just accepts — *"This is what you do to be clean, to be pretty, to be right."*

And maybe that would've saved me from the shame in that moment. Maybe I wouldn't have been pointed at. Maybe no teacher would've told me to cover up.

But it would've come at a different cost.

Because I know myself now. And I know that shaving back then wouldn't have been about choice — it would've been about erasing myself to make other people more comfortable. Altering my body's appearance just to please men. Just to avoid judgment. Just to survive.

And I would've carried that regret. Not because I dislike body hair, but because it wouldn't have been my decision. It would've been theirs.

That's the part no one tells you — that sometimes, shame disguises itself as guidance. And sometimes, survival asks you to disappear.

Freshman year, I was still in that rural town. Still surrounded by the same familiar streets, the same small school, the same expectations that had followed me since childhood. But things at home were starting to fall apart. My parents were heading toward divorce, and even though no one said it out loud, I could feel the cracks forming long before the paperwork began.

Sophomore year, everything changed.

My dad had custody by then, and we had moved to the city. New people, new school, new pressure. No one here knew who I was — and that should have felt like freedom. But it didn't. It felt like performance. Like every hallway I walked was a stage and I didn't know the lines to the character I was supposed to be.

I started going to counseling that year. I remember sitting in that first session, heart racing, hoping — maybe even begging — that the counselor would just *know*. That she'd pull it out of me, gently, like a splinter. She asked me directly: *"Do you feel like a girl?"*

And I lied.
I said no.

Not because it was true.
But because I was scared of what would happen if I told the truth.

The thought that echoed in my head was sharp and constant:
Would this be used to hurt my mom during the divorce?
Would they say she knew? That she caused it? That she made me this way?

I wasn't just protecting myself.
I was trying to protect her, too.

That same year, I got my driver's license. I was in the DMV with my dad, going through the paperwork. When he checked the box for *male*, it felt like a punch to the gut. I wanted to scream. *No — I'm a girl. Check the female box.* But I didn't.

Instead, I stood there in silence while a piece of paper claimed ownership over something I hadn't given permission for. Another layer of hiding. Another layer of being erased.

Later that year, I decided to try out for basketball.

I don't know why, exactly. Maybe I thought it would help me fit in. Maybe I just wanted to do *something*. But when I showed up, the girls were holding cheerleading tryouts in the same gym.

They were lining up, stretching, laughing, flipping their hair. All I could think was, *I wish the world saw me as a girl so I could be over there instead.*

Cheerleading felt beautiful. Bright. Fun.
Basketball just felt... loud. Angry. Rough.
It wasn't about the sport. It was about who belonged where.

The boys at tryouts were aggressive — too aggressive. They shoved, elbowed, cursed. Some of them were trying to prove they were tough. Others were just trying to hurt somebody. I didn't play like that. I didn't want to.

By the end of the tryout, I was cut.

And I remember standing there, sweaty and sore and trying not to let it show. Trying not to care. But deep down, I couldn't help but wonder —
Did the coach see something? Did I play "like a girl"?
Is that why I didn't make the team?

It wasn't just rejection.
It felt like confirmation — that no matter how hard I tried, I would always end up in the wrong room.

Junior year, the hiding got deeper. It stopped being about playing along — it became about staying safe.

That was the year I started vocational classes, held in a larger city. It should've felt like opportunity. It should've felt like progress. Instead, it felt like danger.

Some of the students there didn't just dislike gay people — they hunted them. The things they said about queer kids weren't just cruel, they were *threatening*. And no one stopped them. No one said, "That's enough." It was open season.

I remember thinking:
If this is what they do to gay students... what would they do to me?

What would they do to someone who feels like a girl but looks like a boy?

So I learned to hide better.

That same year, I was forced to take gym class — which meant using the boys' locker room. No stalls. No curtains. No walls. Just rows of benches, and eyes.

By then, I had developed almost fully. My breasts were visible. My chest was soft. My body didn't match the one I was being told to undress like everyone else. Every time I stepped into that room, it didn't feel like a locker room — it felt like a cage.

And I knew it wasn't where I belonged.

Back in freshman year, I had started having hot flashes — waves of heat that made no sense at the time but felt undeniable. That was my body's first whisper that something was different. That I wasn't a boy. That I was in the wrong place.

So standing in that locker room, surrounded by boys who never flinched, never second-guessed, never hid...

I didn't just feel uncomfortable.

I felt **exiled** — like I had been sentenced to a life that didn't fit, just because my truth didn't show up in the right box.

So I found a way to survive:

I started wearing my gym clothes *under* my regular clothes.

That way I could change without undressing.

That way I didn't have to peel myself down to nothing.

That way, at least one part of me wouldn't feel violated.

It wasn't comfort.

It was armor.

And every day, I got better at disappearing.

Gym class wasn't all locker rooms and forced games. Sometimes, we got to pick our own activities. The teacher would list a few options — weight training, flag football, CPR — and let us choose.

One of the weeks, CPR was on the list. And all the girls picked it.

So I did too.

I didn't even think about it. I just moved toward the group like it was natural. And for a moment — a small, fragile moment — it *felt* natural. Like I was where I was supposed to be. Like I belonged there.

Nobody else saw it that way. To them, I was just another student picking an elective.

But to me, it was the first time I felt like I was one of the girls — even if I was the only one who knew it.

By senior year, I had become a master at hiding.

I knew how to move through the day without drawing too much attention. I knew how to dress, how to answer questions, how to pretend I was fine. Teachers wanted me to start thinking about college, so I picked marketing. It seemed safe. Acceptable. Normal. And I had learned that *normal* was the only thing anyone wanted from me.

Then came prom.

And I wanted to go. God, I wanted to go. I wanted to pick out a dress, not a tux. I wanted to have my hair done, nails done, makeup that made me glow. I didn't care about being a queen or a date or the center of attention. I just wanted to feel beautiful.

I didn't go to prom.

The voice in my head was louder than any invitation. It wasn't mine — it was my father's. *"You have to look normal. You have to be normal."*

He had said it to me more times than I could count. It had been instilled in me for years — long before high school, long before I even had the language to explain who I was.

So instead of going to prom, I went to work.

I was a cashier. Most of the cashiers were girls — sweet, smiling, friendly girls. And that night, I was one of them. Secretly. Silently. I wore my uniform, scanned barcodes, counted change, and *glowed* on the inside.

Because that was my prom.

No heels. No slow dances. No corsage.
But I had my smile. I had my space. I had my quiet joy.
And for one night, I wasn't pretending to be normal.

I was just being me.

Graduation prep came fast. We lined up for caps and gowns, ready to rehearse the moment we'd all been waiting for.

The girls wore white. The boys wore red.

I wanted so badly to wear white. I didn't care about walking across a stage or shaking hands with administrators who never really knew me. I just wanted that gown. That quiet signal that I was like them. That maybe, even for one day, the world would see me as I was.

But no.

I was forced to wear red.

I accepted it — told myself it didn't matter, that graduation was about what came next. That soon I'd be free.

New chapter. New life. No more hiding.

Boy, was I in for a shock.

Looking back at those years, there's something I need to say — something I've carried with me in silence for far too long.

To the girls I attempted to date… I'm sorry.

At the time, I didn't realize the harm my pretending may have caused. I didn't know how much pain I was placing in someone else's hands just by trying to survive. But now, I can see it.

I wasn't dating out of love — I was dating out of fear.
I used those relationships to appear "normal" to the outside world. To prove something I didn't even believe. And that makes me feel disgusted with myself.

I didn't mean to hurt anyone. But I know I did.

And that knowledge doesn't sit lightly.

So if you're reading this — if you remember me — I want you to know this isn't a confession. It's an apology.

From someone who was lost, hiding, and trying desperately to be someone they weren't —
I am truly sorry.

And that was the cruelest part of all:
She was always there. She just had to hide in plain sight.

College after high school was short-lived.

I had enrolled in a marketing program, mostly because it seemed safe — professional, neutral, respectable. Something I could say out loud without anyone asking too many questions. But my heart wasn't in it. Not even close.

Still, there was something oddly comforting about that classroom. I hadn't expected to feel anything — just get through the credits and pretend to care. But what caught me off guard was the number of young women in the class. Bright, hopeful, focused. I didn't talk to many of them, but being surrounded by them — just existing in the same space — gave me a strange sense of peace. Like I had wandered into the right room, even if I was still pretending I didn't belong there.

But I didn't last long.

A month in, I dropped out.

I quit my job at Walmart too — not because I wanted to, but because I had to. My living situation collapsed, and I had no choice but to move in with my mom… in another state. It wasn't ideal. I wasn't ready to start over again. But the one thing I knew for sure was that I couldn't stay and face my dad after dropping out.

I didn't want to hear the disappointment in his voice.
I didn't want to feel like a failure again — not in front of him.
I'd spent years performing, pretending, making myself small just to fit his version of what I was supposed to be.

So I ran.

But when you're running from something that lives inside you… you never really get away.

Living with my mother didn't last long either.

Her boyfriend at the time was controlling, cruel — the kind of man who could turn a dinner table into a battlefield with just a glare. I barely lasted two weeks under that roof before he forced me out. No warning. No backup plan.

And just like that, I was on my own.

I ended up living in my car — parked in the same Walmart lot I had once worked in. I used to clock in at that store, wearing a name tag and trying to pretend I was normal. Now I was sleeping in the backseat under tinted windows, hoping no one would knock or look too closely.

Every night was a balancing act between being invisible and staying safe.

I fell in with the wrong group of friends around that time — not because I didn't know better, but because I didn't have the luxury of better.

When you're sleeping in your car, the bar for safety gets lower and lower until anything that isn't violent starts to feel like company.

And besides… pretending to belong had become second nature by then.

Hanging with that group of friends eventually caught up with me.

It finally paid off — in the worst way possible.

I landed in trouble with the law. Nothing glamorous. Nothing worth the cost. Just another consequence of drifting through life without a place to anchor. I wasn't dangerous — just lost. But the system doesn't always care about the difference.

What saved me wasn't a clean record or a good lawyer. It was a dying wish.

My grandmother — on my father's side — was sick. Cancer. It had taken over her body and was slowly stealing what was left of her strength.

But even in that state, she did something that changed the direction of my life.

She begged my Aunt Lisa to take me in.

And Aunt Lisa did.

Aunt Lisa's home turned out to be the best place for me.

It wasn't perfect. It wasn't soft. But it was safe — and after everything I had been through, that was enough.

She had known me since I was little. During my early childhood, Aunt Lisa had seen firsthand what the bullies and the school system were doing to me. She didn't just hear about it — she *knew*. She saw the bruises, the avoidance, the silence I carried around like a second backpack.

And she did what no one else had ever done: she taught me to fight back.

Not just with words — with fists if I had to. "Take no crap," she said. "If they hit, you hit harder." She wasn't raising me to be violent. She was raising me to *stop being a target*. For the first time, someone wasn't asking me to shrink — they were giving me permission to stand.

And that permission, even when rough around the edges, gave me a kind of strength I didn't know I had.

But Aunt Lisa wasn't all toughness and bark.

She had a soft side, too — one that showed up in the quiet moments, the little teachings she passed on without fanfare. One of her core beliefs, one I still carry to this day, was simple:

"Be kind to all living things."

She didn't preach it. She lived it. Whether it was an injured animal, a struggling neighbor, or just a plant that needed watering — she showed care in a way that didn't ask for attention. It was just who she was.

Aunt Lisa had lived a hard life. The world hadn't made space for her to exist easily. She was a lesbian, and she didn't hide it. Her relationship wasn't whispered about — it was real, open, *visible*. In a world that tried to silence women like her, she stayed loud anyway.

And in that house — with her, and her partner, and their rules of kindness and strength — I found something I hadn't felt in a long time.

I found the edges of home.

While living at Aunt Lisa's, things started to stabilize — at least on the surface.

I managed to get a job at Home Depot. It wasn't exactly where I wanted to be. I had hoped to land something as a cashier — something front-end, something closer to the kind of femininity I had always admired from the sidelines. But at that point, any job was a win. I needed money.

I needed purpose. I needed a reason to wake up and pretend things were okay.

And pretending had become my specialty.

One day at the mall, everything shifted — not publicly, not loudly, but *inside me*.

I came across a copy of the Filene's catalog. I don't know why I picked it up at first. Maybe curiosity. Maybe fate. But there it was — page after page of women's clothing, accessories, lingerie. Not just fabric — *possibility*. I flipped through it slowly, like each turn of the page was a secret I wasn't supposed to know.

And then… I did it.

I placed an order.

Shapewear. From the women's section. For me.

My hands were shaking as I filled out the form. The catalog said "standard shipping," but to me it felt like I was sending a message to the universe.

A message that said, *She's still here. She hasn't given up.*

The feeling that came over me as I sealed the envelope was something I'll never forget.

It was *exciting*.
It was *terrifying*.
It was *mine*.

The package came in the mail a few days later.

I remember holding it like it was fragile — like the box might shatter if I breathed too hard.

It felt like Christmas morning, except no one else knew the holiday was happening. Just me. Just this little box of truth, wrapped in plain brown paper.

I slipped into the bathroom with it tucked under my arm, heart pounding. Locked the door. Turned the fan on. Sat on the edge of the tub. I opened it slowly — not because I didn't know what was inside, but because I *did*.

Shapewear.

Soft, sleek, beautiful. The fabric hugged my fingers as I pulled it from the box. It wasn't just clothing. It was a *signal*. A whisper that said, *This is who you are.*

And my body — oh God, my body *knew.*

It reacted instantly. Not with shame, not with fear. With **joy**. Pure, overwhelming joy.

My chest swelled with it. My heart raced. I fell in love. With the fabric. With the moment. With myself.

Then something deeper took over — an instinct, a pull I couldn't ignore.

Try them on.

It wasn't a thought. It was a command. Something inside me *needed* to feel it, to see it, to confirm that it was real.

So I did.

I stepped into the shapewear like I was stepping into *me*. And for one brief, beautiful moment, everything felt right. Like the world had stopped arguing with me. Like the war between body and mind had called a truce.

I looked in the mirror, and I didn't feel like a stranger.

I felt *seen* — by myself.

But it didn't last.

The moment passed, and the fear rushed in —
that old, heavy fear I had carried for so long.
This isn't normal.
What if someone finds out?
**What if this means something you're not ready
to face?**

I peeled the shapewear off, folded it carefully,
and tucked it away like contraband.

Not because it was wrong.

But because I had been taught to believe *I was*.

I lived with Aunt Lisa for about a year.

A full year of safety, quiet strength, and small,
secret steps toward who I was becoming. It wasn't
always easy, but for the first time in a long time, I
didn't feel like I was surviving alone.

And then the news came — the kind that hits low and leaves you breathless.

Aunt Lisa and her partner were moving out of state.

I didn't cry. I didn't beg them to stay. I just stood there and nodded, pretending I understood. Pretending it didn't feel like the ground had been yanked out from beneath me.

But inside… I was unraveling.

This was the first place in years that had felt like a home — not just a roof, but a *refuge*. And now it was slipping through my fingers, and I had no idea what came next.

Once again, I was being asked to pretend I was okay.

And once again, I did what I had always done:

I disappeared behind the mask.

I wish I had told her.

I wish I had found the courage to sit Aunt Lisa down and say it out loud — to tell her who I really was, how I truly felt, and what I was carrying behind the smile and silence.

But I didn't.

I kept it tucked away, hidden beneath the same layers I had worn for years. Not because I didn't

trust her — but because I didn't trust the world not to punish me for it.

I thought I had time.

Time to explain.
Time to share.
Time to show her the woman she had helped keep alive.

But that time never came.

Aunt Lisa is gone now.

And with her went one of the few people who might have understood — who might have hugged me a little tighter, told me she already knew, and reminded me that being kind to all living things included *being kind to myself.*

I'll never get that moment back.

But I carry her with me.

In every breath I take as Ashley.
In every step I walk in truth.
In every act of softness I refuse to apologize for.

She taught me how to fight — and how to feel.

And even though I never got to say it to her face…

I think she knew.

Chapter 6: Darkness Lies Ahead

Before Aunt Lisa left, I had one last meeting with my mother.

It had been a while. A lot had happened. But this time, something was different — *we were different.* Maybe it was the distance. Maybe it was time. Maybe it was watching me fall so far outside the safety net that she couldn't ignore it anymore.

She knew I had been living in my car. I hadn't tried to hide it. And in a strange twist of pain and solidarity, she spent that first week *right beside me* — parking her own car next to mine, sleeping in it just like I was.

Two women in two vehicles, trying

to find warmth and safety in a world that offered neither.

It wasn't glamorous. It wasn't noble. It was survival — and it was all we had.

Eventually, she agreed to let me move back in. Not out of pity. Out of love. Quiet, cautious love — but love all the same.

But home wasn't safe. Not yet.

That same scumbag boyfriend was still there. Still draining her energy. Still stealing the money that was supposed to go to rent. Still twisting his control into every corner of the house.

So we made a pact — me and my mother.

He was going… or we were.

We were done surviving separately. This time, we'd survive together.

When we got back to my mom's apartment, it was time to draw the line.

We laid down the ground rules — not in whispers, not in hints. **Direct. Unmistakable.** There would be no confusion. No more dancing around dysfunction. No more pretending we didn't see what was happening.

This wasn't a negotiation.

Dave — her boyfriend — the same man who had forced me out before, the same one bleeding her dry emotionally and financially, was either **leaving**…

Or we were.

There was no in-between. No "let's see how it goes."
We were done shrinking ourselves for his comfort.

For the first time in a long time, my mother and I were on the same side — not just biologically, but emotionally. And that made us dangerous.

Dave made his choice.

He stayed.

There wasn't a scene. There didn't need to be. The silence said it all — the way he brushed off the ultimatum, the way he lit up with his buddies like nothing was happening, like our boundaries were just background noise.

But we weren't bluffing.

A couple days later, while he was getting stoned in the living room, laughing like the world still belonged to him, **we rented a U-Haul**.

We had already put down the deposit on a new apartment. Already packed the essentials. Already planned our escape. We didn't need to wait for his answer — we *knew* what it was going to be.

So we took what was ours and left him with nothing but his smoke and his ego.

He stayed.

We didn't.

Things were starting to look good.

We had our own apartment. The air felt different — lighter, like we had cleared just enough of the wreckage to breathe again. I was working, keeping my head down, trying to build something stable.
And then it happened:

I got promoted.

Cashier.
The role I had wanted all along. The one that always felt quietly affirming — like a glimpse into the version of myself I wasn't allowed to be. It wasn't just a better position. It was a better feeling.

I stood behind that register, smiling, scanning, standing beside women who felt like reflections of something I couldn't fully reach — but could almost touch. It made me feel like I belonged… even if no one around me understood why.

But not all was what it seemed.

Because the world doesn't let girls like me win without a price.

And the darkness… was already on its way.

The darkness took me by surprise.

Not slowly. Not subtly.
It came quickly. Swiftly. Like a thief in the night, pulling the rug out just as I was starting to feel steady on my feet.

It started with a dull, achy pain — nothing dramatic, just enough to make me pause. Enough to make work uncomfortable.

Enough to make me wonder if maybe I'd just pulled something or slept wrong.

But it didn't go away.

It lingered. Spread. Deepened.

And soon I was in a hospital gown, laying under bright white lights while a nurse prepped me for a **CT scan** — checking for **appendicitis**.

It felt like a joke.
I had just started to rise, to find rhythm, to feel *okay…*
And now my body was becoming the battlefield again.

I returned home a few hours later, relieved to be out of the fluorescent lights and hospital silence.

But then the phone rang.

It was the follow-up call — the results from the CAT scan. The voice on the other end was calm, clinical, routine.

Everything looked normal.

Nothing abnormal was found.

I stood there, frozen, the phone pressed against my ear like it might deliver better news if I held it tighter.

All I could think was:

You must be wrong.

Because this pain?

This wasn't imagined.

It wasn't fake.

It was real enough to drive me to the ER. Real enough to make me afraid. Real enough to shatter the illusion that I was finally safe.

So if it wasn't my appendix…
Then what *was* it?

That question lingered longer than the pain itself.

The pain didn't end with that scan.

A few weeks passed — maybe a month — and it returned.

Not with the same fury, but enough to make me stop in my tracks. A dull, familiar ache in the same place: lower right abdomen, the spot where they say the appendix lives. It wasn't enough to send me back to the hospital, but it was enough to haunt me.

This time, it brought company.

I started having back pain too — low, persistent, and hard to explain. Like something was tugging from the inside out. It didn't scream. It whispered.

But it whispered loud enough to follow me to work, to keep me up at night, to remind me that something wasn't right.

And yet… there was still no answer.

No swelling. No fever. No "medical emergency" the doctors could see.

But I could feel it.

Right side. Always the right side. Always where the appendix is supposed to be. But they said mine was fine — "unremarkable," as they liked to say.

Funny how a body can be unremarkable on paper and still feel like it's falling apart in real life.

I started wondering if maybe I was the problem. If maybe the pain was in my head. If maybe I just wanted attention — the kind of toxic thoughts that crawl in when the world doesn't believe your body.

But I knew better.

I knew my body wasn't lying.

It just wasn't speaking in a language anyone else could understand.

The pain didn't follow a schedule — but it followed a pattern.

Some months, it barely made a sound. Just a whisper. A twinge. Something I could ignore if I distracted myself enough.

Other times, it roared.

Sharp. Radiating. Enough to curl me over. Enough to make me question if I was about to collapse at work, on the floor, in front of everyone. It always came back to the same place — my lower right side, where the appendix sits.

The first time, they scanned me. Found nothing. The second time, same thing — nothing.

But when the pain flared up a third time, bad enough to send me back to the ER, I had a thought:

Maybe it's not the hospital. Maybe it's the scanner. The way they're using it. The assumptions they're making.

So I tried something new.

A different hospital. Different intake forms. Different technicians. Maybe a different set of eyes would finally see what mine already knew:

Something was wrong.

But again… the scan came back clean.

Unremarkable. Normal. Male.

And that's when something inside me broke — not with despair, but with clarity.

A lightbulb moment.

They're scanning me like a man.

They're not finding the problem… because they're not looking for it.

Because my body isn't playing by the rules they expect — and neither is my pain.

And then, for the first time, I said it to myself with full certainty:

I must be a woman.

Not in theory.
Not in identity alone.
But in body. In blood. In the rhythm of something deeper.

Because I wasn't just having random flare-ups — I was cycling.

Month to month, the pattern repeated. A rise. A fall. A rhythm. Pain that came and went like clockwork. Emotional shifts I could chart like a calendar.

I began to feel what I could only describe as hormonal tides — low points that made me snappy, sensitive, irritable. Like everything was made of sandpaper.

And then the highs — days when the fog lifted and I felt incredible. Confident. Electric. Like my skin fit perfectly and I could take on the world.

That wasn't coincidence.
That was estrogen.

I could feel it in my bloodstream — like a warm current moving through me. Subtle, but unmistakable. And when it surged, I didn't just feel good… I felt *right.*

This wasn't some psychosomatic fantasy. This wasn't me wanting to be a woman and making it all up to match the dream.

This was biology.

This was *my* biology.

And suddenly, everything made sense.

The pain managed to drive me back to the hospital yet again.

But this time… was different.

This time, there was blood.

Not imagined. Not invisible. Real. Tangible. Proof.

I remember thinking, *There's no way they can miss this. Not now. Not with this.*

But I was wrong.

They ran tests. Took scans. Poked, prodded, searched.

And still — nothing.

They even scheduled a colonoscopy, hoping maybe the answer was hiding somewhere deeper, somewhere less obvious.

But it turned up clean.

Just like all the rest.

And I was left with the same echo I'd been trying to silence for months:

They're not going to find it… because they're not looking for her.

I thought this was my rock bottom.

Laying in that hospital bed, bleeding, confused, dismissed once again — I told myself it couldn't get any worse. That this was the lowest it could go. That at least now, with everything I'd been through, the only direction left… was up.

But I had forgotten something.

Something I was taught once — a quiet truth buried deep in the back of my mind:

A bulb burns brightest before it blows.

And I was glowing.

Flickering.

About to shatter.

⚠ Trigger Warning

If you can't handle seeing a person stripped to
their core —
beaten, bared, and bruised —
this chapter is not for you.

Sitting in my primary care doctor's office,
another round of pain weighing down my body like
wet cement, I barely moved.

Not because I was tired — because I was afraid.
Afraid that moving even slightly might make it
worse.
Afraid of flinching. Afraid of proving again that
something was wrong that no one could explain.

The door opened. My doctor walked in.

Clipboard in hand. Calm, polite.
She looked at me — saw the tension, the
discomfort, the barely-contained pain — and
offered what she must've thought was mercy.

Painkillers.

A magic pill. A chemical pause button. A way to
silence my body, not heal it.

That was the cure they kept offering.

Not answers. Not belief.
Just the option to numb myself long enough to stop
being a burden.

She told me she believed me.

That she didn't think I was faking it. That she
could see I was in pain.
Then she handed me two things:

A referral…

And a prescription.

Painkillers.

No diagnosis. No theory. No real conversation about *why* this kept happening.

Just: *Here, take this.*

Like I was a machine with a jammed gear, and the fix was to dull the grinding until it wasn't so loud anymore.

I didn't argue. I didn't push back.

I nodded, thanked her, and walked out with the little slip of paper in my hand.

Because what else was I supposed to do?

I didn't feel seen.

I felt packaged. Processed. Stamped.

Like a piece of meat in a meat factory — examined, labeled, pushed down the line.

And whatever part of me was still screaming on the inside…

wasn't anyone's concern but mine.

At the time, I had just started a new job — concrete inspector.

It wasn't exactly a job most people imagined a woman doing.
But I liked it.

I liked the structure, the routine, the problem-solving. I liked being out in the field, traveling from site to site. Every day was different. I got to see new places, do real work, touch something permanent.

Concrete was honest.
It cracked or it didn't.
It passed or it failed.
There was no pretending.

Maybe that's why I liked it so much.

In a world where I was constantly questioned —
where my body was a mystery, my pain was a
puzzle, and my truth was always being debated —
at least *the concrete told the truth.*

Around that time, I started seeing a counselor.

Not because I was ready to open up —
but because the pain was leaking into everything.
And people thought therapy might help.

But I didn't tell them the truth.

I couldn't.

I was too afraid of what they'd label me if I did.
Crazy. Confused. Delusional.

So I lied.

I told them what they wanted to hear — just
enough to make it seem like progress, just enough
to keep the appointments going.

I gave them scraps while hiding the core. Out of fear. Out of habit. Out of survival.

After a while, it became a game.

Every new counselor was another round.
I'd sit down in their office, scan the room, and quietly ask myself:

Who's going to crack the walnut first?

None of them did.

They made it too easy. Their lives were all over their offices — wedding photos, diplomas, inspirational quotes, kids' drawings taped to their bookshelves.
They didn't know I was studying them as much as they were studying me.

They thought I was opening up.

But I was building walls with a smile.

It all started taking its toll.

The pain was one thing — but the painkillers? They came with a cost.

They dulled the edge, sure.
But they dulled *everything else*, too.

I started feeling reckless on the job. Zoned out. Sluggish. There were moments on the worksite where I wasn't fully present — and when you're working around heavy equipment and deadlines, that's not just dangerous. It's a liability.

The doctor visits didn't help either. Or the counseling appointments.
They were constant. Disruptive. Endless.
Every week I was explaining myself to another stranger while my real life — my job — started slipping through my hands.

I couldn't keep up.

The job that had made me feel strong… started slipping away.

So I quit.

It wasn't some dramatic walk-off. It was quiet. Shameful.
Like admitting I had lost a fight I wasn't even supposed to be in.

And when the paychecks stopped and the symptoms didn't, I was left with no choice:

I applied for SSDI.

I wasn't proud of it.
But pride doesn't keep the lights on.

And at that point, I didn't have anything left but pain, paperwork, and the hope that maybe — just maybe — someone would finally believe me.

A month passed.

Then the letter came.

Social Security — the decision.

I opened it with shaky hands, holding my breath without realizing it.

Denied.

How?

The state I lived in had already declared me *totally and permanently disabled*. They used the same kind of doctors, the same evaluators, the same framework. Their decision wasn't quick or impulsive — it was based on what they saw, what they knew.

And what they saw was everything I had stopped seeing in myself.

They saw the decline — the unwashed hair, the neglected clothes, the hollowed-out version of someone who used to have pride in how she looked.

They saw the way I barely made eye contact, how I flinched at questions, how I moved like someone trying not to exist.

They saw the isolation.
The absence.
The slow erosion of a person trying to hold on.

But Social Security?

They didn't see any of it.

Or maybe they just didn't care.

To them, I was just another number. Another file to stamp.

And whatever truth I was living in —
they couldn't see it.

I did the only thing I thought I could do.

I retained one of those Social Security lawyers — the kind you see on TV or on the back of a bus bench.

No money upfront. No risk, really. Just a sliver of possibility.

What did I have to lose?

I was already denied. Already sinking. Already living in a body that didn't work and a world that didn't want to see it.

So I signed the papers.
Made the call.
Gave them permission to speak on my behalf.

And we filed the appeal.

It wasn't a victory. It wasn't even hope.
It was just… *something.*
A move. A response. A breath against the weight.

Waiting for that appeal would become its own kind of torment.

Because survival didn't pause just because the paperwork was in.

Aunt Lisa had moved back to the state a few years earlier.

She'd finally bought a house — a quiet place with a yard, some stability.
She even got a dog — a massive Great Dane named Fenway, who acted like a toddler trapped in a tank's body. Gentle. Loyal. Goofy. The kind of dog that could melt your heart just by existing.

Part of me wanted to visit.
To feel that comfort again. To feel *her* again.

But I stayed away.

Because my cousin was there.

He had a drug problem — one that didn't just stay in his veins.
He brought it into every room. Every conversation. Every chance he could find to manipulate the people who still cared about him.

The last time I visited, he pulled me aside like he wanted to talk — said he was hurting, said he needed help.

But he didn't want help.

He wanted my painkillers.

And when I said no?

He turned on me. Fast.
Said I was selfish. Said I didn't understand.
Said things that cut deep — not because they were true, but because they were designed to hit where I was already bleeding.

I left that day feeling like trash. Not just because of what he said… but because of what it revealed:

That even around family, I couldn't let my guard down.

Even in a house with a dog named Fenway and a woman who once helped save me…

I wasn't safe.

Eventually, Aunt Lisa found out the truth.

My cousin — the one I had avoided, the one who had once tried to guilt me out of my own prescription — had taken things even further.

She caught him bringing strange men into her home. Not friends. Not partners. Clients. He had turned her house into something she never agreed to — something dangerous, humiliating, and deeply disrespectful.

And it wasn't just the downstairs.
He was living in the second-floor apartment — the one Aunt Lisa owned. Because the house wasn't just her home. It was a **two-family**, and she was the landlord.

The roommates upstairs had been handing him their rent money, trusting him to pay the bills.
But he didn't.

He spent it — all of it — on drugs, on whatever filled the void he refused to face.

And Lisa had had enough.

He was on his way out.

That's when she called me.
Offered me a chance.
A room upstairs. A new start. A door that wasn't slamming shut.

And I said yes.

Part of it was survival. But part of it — the deeper part — was about coming full circle.

Years earlier, when my brother had moved in with me and my mom, he had taken over the living room. We made it work. It wasn't ideal, but we found a way to share what little we had.

Now it was my turn to do the same.

I offered my room to him.

And I moved in upstairs — not just into a new space, but back into Lisa's orbit.
Back into the one place that had once felt like safety.

Even if I didn't know what would come next, I knew one thing:

I was finally in a house where the locks didn't feel like a warning.

I had lost everything I thought made me strong — my job, my health, my independence.
And just when the darkness felt total… a door opened.
But safety doesn't erase suffering.
And even in this new place, with a lock that didn't warn me, I still carried every bruise inside.
I wasn't healed.

I was just… **sheltered long enough to survive what came next.**

🐾 Take a Breath

Before you begin this chapter…

Put the phone down.

Take a breath.

Exhale slowly.

And if you're someone who cries easily — maybe grab a tissue.

This is the part where grief walks in.

The part that's quiet, but heavy.

The part I didn't want to write — but had to.

Because this is the chapter where a hero dies.

A month into living at Lisa's, things were finally starting to look up.

The apartment was warm, quiet, stable.
Fenway — her Great Dane — was my shadow, a giant with a gentle soul and terrible boundaries. He had no idea he wasn't a lap dog.
For the first time in what felt like years, I could breathe.

Then another letter arrived.
Social Security.

I spotted it in the mail slot — crumpled, damp, and already half-destroyed.

Fenway had gotten to it first.

True to form, he shredded that sucker like it owed him rent.

His instincts were right.

It was another denial.

I stood there holding the remains of the letter, more confetti than paperwork, and realized something: *This system isn't broken. It's rigged.*

They weren't just denying me because they didn't believe me.
They were denying me because they didn't want to pay me.
Because if they approved the appeal, they'd owe me *back pay.* A lump sum. Months of benefits retroactively.

So I did what survivors do.

I didn't scream.
I didn't break down.
I filed a new claim — started the process all over again.

Because that's what it felt like. A game of delay. A way to wear people down until they stopped asking.

But I wasn't stopping.

Not yet.

About a week into waiting, I started feeling restless.

I didn't want to be a bum.
Didn't want to be a leech.
Didn't want to become *him* — my cousin — circling addiction and excuses while everyone around him picked up the pieces.

So I did what felt honest.

I applied for a job as a cashier.

It wasn't glamorous. But it was familiar —
something that had once given me pride, structure,
and just enough human connection to keep me
grounded.
And besides, being zoned out on painkillers while
running a register felt a lot safer than doing field
work or driving across the state.

I leaned into the roots of who I used to be.

And they took me back.

I got hired.

A uniform. A schedule. A reason to get out of
bed.
It didn't fix anything — not really. But it was
movement.
And after everything I'd lost, movement felt like
hope.

Three days into training — just as I was starting
to feel human again — my phone buzzed.

I was in the back room, sitting at the training computer, halfway through a tutorial on price overrides and coupon scanning. Just another box to check on the road back to normal.

I glanced at the screen.

And I knew.

I don't remember the exact words. I don't remember if I answered or just stared.

But I remember what it felt like.

The dread phone call.

The one that still scars my brain.
The one that ripped the air out of the room without a sound.
The one that brought the kind of silence you can't explain to anyone who hasn't heard it.

The day the music died.

It was my dad.

I answered.

His voice was strained, already halfway broken. *"Something happened to Lisa. They're taking her to the hospital."*

That was all I needed to hear.

I jumped up, heart slamming into my ribs, legs already moving before my mind could catch up.

I ran to the punch clock.
My hands were shaking. I couldn't even figure out how to clock out. A simple task — tap, tap, done — suddenly felt impossible. My fingers kept missing. The numbers blurred.

Everything was spinning.

Once I finally got out, I bolted to the parking lot — heart in my throat, vision tunneled, adrenaline pounding through me like a war drum.

I got in the car, slammed it into drive.

Speed limits didn't matter.

Trash cans? Get out of the way.

Everything — and I mean everything — was in my way.

Nothing was going to stop me.

I was going to the hospital.

To Lisa.

To my hero.

I made it to the hospital, parked like a maniac, and ran straight to the reception desk.

I didn't stop to breathe. Didn't bother with politeness.

"Where is Lisa's room?" I blurted, already bracing myself for the worst.

The woman behind the counter looked up calmly and said, *"One moment, please."*

She clicked around on her screen.

Too slow.

Everything too slow.

Then she said it.

"We have no record of a Lisa here."

My stomach dropped.

I blinked. Hard.

What do you mean, no record?

I asked again. She double-checked. Nothing.

And in that moment, something in me fractured.

Thirty minutes had passed since the call.

Thirty minutes was long enough for everything to change.

My brain — lightning-fast, unwilling but unstoppable — started connecting the dots.

She wasn't here because she'd never been admitted.

Because it was already too late.

Because there was no need for a room.

I didn't wait.
Didn't argue.

I turned and walked out of the building, my feet barely touching the ground.

I didn't need anyone to say it.

I already knew.

I felt cursed.

I managed to get back home.

I didn't drive fast this time.
I didn't need to.
Some part of me was still hoping that maybe, if I took my time, the truth would hold off a little longer. That I wouldn't have to hear it out loud.

I pulled into the driveway, heart leaden, limbs heavy.

An aunt was standing on the curb in front of the house.

She didn't say anything at first.

She didn't have to.

I looked at her — and she told me what I already knew.

Lisa was gone.

My mouth started watering.

My gut twisted hard — tight and cruel.

I barely made it to the curb before I dropped to my knees, leaning over a drainage grate and emptying the contents of my stomach into the metal mouth below.

I didn't cry.

Not yet.

I couldn't.

My body broke before my heart could catch up.

Lisa was my hero.

I didn't need to tell her who I was —

she saw me.

She knew me.

And that was enough.

I just wish I'd had the chance to say it out loud.

Lisa was gone.

And just like that, the world kept moving — like it hadn't lost something sacred.

The new job cut me loose like I was spoiled lunch meat. No call. No explanation. Just silence. Maybe they thought I was unstable. Maybe I was. But grief doesn't punch a time clock, and I didn't have anything left to give.

Then came the kicker.

Lisa had written a will — one that left everything to me. The apartment. The dog. The peace I had just started to believe in.

But she never signed it.

All that intention. All that love.
It vanished with the ink she never got to lay down.

And now, the door opened for someone else.

Enter the greedy aunt.

She didn't come to mourn.

She came to take.

She swept in with entitlement, like she had been waiting for this. Like Lisa's death was just an opening in her schedule.

Meanwhile, I was standing there with Fenway — a dog too big to carry but too loyal to leave — remembering the promise I made.

"I'll take care of him," I told her once, without hesitation.
"If anything ever happens, I've got him."

And now something had happened.

And I was holding a promise in one hand, and an eviction in the other.

If *Hungry Hungry Hippos* was ever made into a movie, **Greedy Aunt** would be the lead hippo.

Give me, give me. Feed me, feed me.

She didn't come to grieve.
She came to devour.

And I swear — before the paramedics even arrived, she must have ripped Lisa's necklace straight off her neck. The one Lisa *never* took off. Not even in the shower. Not even in her sleep.

Gone.

Just like that.

The dust hadn't even settled, and she was already scavenging the remains.

Lisa's co-workers had left **gift cards** at her wake — tucked inside envelopes, placed gently on the memorial table. Some had notes. Some didn't. But all of them were meant for **Fenway**.

For his food.
His toys.

His vet care.
His comfort.

Every bit of it was a gesture of love — a promise from the people who knew Lisa best that her dog wouldn't be forgotten.

But Greedy Aunt?

She scooped them up like loose change.

No thank you. No acknowledgment.
Just a quiet grab when no one was looking — like she was entitled to it. Like grief gave her the right to collect.

She didn't even ask where they came from.

She just assumed everything in the room — including Fenway — now belonged to her.

She started *talking about selling Fenway.*
Like he was furniture. Like he was something to list online and cash out on.

Lisa's dog.

The one I promised to care for.

Just another thing on her checklist.

I wasn't going to let her sell Fenway.

Not while Lisa's scent was still on his fur.
Not while the memory of her voice still made his
ears perk up.

But I knew I couldn't fight her directly. She was
greedy, yes — but worse than that, she was
shameless. The kind of person who'd take your
grief and dare you to make a scene about it.

So I got creative.

I started a social media campaign.

I didn't use her name.
Didn't post my face.
Just the story — carefully written, emotional, and
anonymous.

I called it: **Feeding the Hippo.**

At first it was small. A few posts. A few shares.
But it caught on.
People knew exactly the kind of person I was
talking about — because almost everyone had a
"hippo" in their life. The kind who shows up with a
fork and a shopping bag the second someone dies.

It put just enough pressure on her to stop.

To back off.

To realize that Fenway wasn't furniture. He
wasn't for sale.
He wasn't a leftover to be cashed in.

He was a promise.

And she didn't own that. I did.

Greedy Aunt tried to become executor of Lisa's
estate.

Of course she did.

She probably pictured herself standing tall, signing papers, collecting keys — finally getting her hands on something she thought she deserved.

But it didn't work out that way.

She couldn't get bonded.

They don't just hand out that kind of power — not without trust, not without background checks.

And while no one said it out loud…
I couldn't help but wonder if it had something to do with the **bank fraud** she pulled when her own mother died.

Funny how those things have a way of catching up.

She wanted control.
She wanted the title, the authority, the assets.

But the system — the same one that had failed *me* so many times — finally shut her out.

And for once, it felt like the universe was paying attention.

But Greedy Aunt wasn't done.

There was still **Lisa's life insurance**.

Lisa had told me — clearly, intentionally — that she had added me as the beneficiary. It wasn't a guess. It wasn't a hope. It was something she *said out loud* with conviction.

But when the paperwork came through?

I wasn't on it.

No trace. No mention. Just… gone.

Something didn't smell right.

And then I found out Greedy Aunt had made friends in **Lisa's old HR department** — the same department that handled benefits, policies, and change forms.

Cute.

I don't think so, Hungry Hippo.

You're not taking that.

This wasn't just greed anymore. This was fraud. Quiet, subtle, maybe even legal-looking — but I knew what it was. And I wasn't going to roll over and let her cash in on Lisa's death while pretending she earned it.

So I made noise.

The kind of noise that insurance companies don't like.

I filed a report.
I called.
I documented everything I had.
I used my voice — the one Lisa helped me find — and I refused to go quiet.

I don't know what they found.

They never tell you everything.

But I know this: the payout didn't come easy.

And that hippo?

She didn't get to feed.

Then, finally, something shifted.

I got a packet in the mail — thick, official-looking. My name typed neatly on the front. Inside: **proof**.

I was listed as a **beneficiary**.

Lisa *had* added me.

She wasn't mistaken.

She wasn't just saying it to comfort me.

It was real.

And now it was recognized.

That same week, a second letter came.

Social Security.

Approved.

After all the denials, all the appeals, all the months of silence — they finally approved me.

And just like I suspected from the beginning…
It was never about the pain.
It was about the payout.

They didn't want to backdate the benefits.
Didn't want to hand over that lump sum.

But they lost that game.

Because I didn't stop fighting.

And suddenly, in the middle of grief and ashes, I had proof — not just that the system had failed me, but that I had been **right** to scream.

For the first time in a long time, I can finally see a light at the end of the tunnel.
It's faint.
It's far.

But it's real.

And this time… it's not a train.

Chapter 10: A Concrete Foundation

Greedy Aunt wasn't done playing **Hungry Hungry Hippo**.

She thought she had one more trick up her sleeve.

She started whispering to the other heirs — painting Lisa's house like it was some kind of **mega million jackpot**. Her story? That the property was worth a fortune, and they were all about to cash in.

What she left out, of course, was that **the mortgage was higher than the home's value**.
It wasn't a gold mine.
It was underwater.

But logic never stopped a feeding frenzy.

Meanwhile, I had an **iron-clad lease**.

Lisa had signed it — clear as day — giving me **tenant rights to the second-floor apartment** at **$0 per month**. It wasn't a loophole. It was her *intention*. She wanted me to have a home. She wanted Fenway to stay where he belonged.

I tried to do the right thing.

I even looked into **transferring the loan** into my name — keeping the house, keeping Fenway's world intact. But it became clear real fast: this wasn't about Lisa anymore.

It was **feeding time**.

So I said **screw it**.

I walked away from the circus, took my life insurance payout, and bought **my own house**.

One with a real foundation. One where **Fenway and I** could start over.

No ghosts.

No vultures.

Just walls I chose — and peace I built.

The house I bought wasn't perfect.

It needed work — walls patched, floors leveled, years of wear peeled back one layer at a time.

But it was **mine**.

And I wasn't in a rush.

I had a plan.

I had time — thanks to the lease Lisa left me. I used it until the very last day. Not to coast, but to prepare. To make sure that when we moved, it wasn't just a change of address.

It was a **new beginning**.

I used those months to make our house a home.

A real one.

A place where there was space for my **mother**, my **brother**, **Fenway**, and me.

Four souls who had been knocked around by life more than once — finally landing under one roof that didn't ask us to apologize for existing.

There was still noise. Still trauma in the walls we carried with us.

But the foundation was solid.

Because this time… we poured it ourselves.

In the privacy of my new bedroom — behind a door that locked, in a house that was mine — **she started coming out more**.

I couldn't hold her back anymore.

I didn't want to.

There was no more Lisa's house. No more Greedy Aunt. No one watching. No one to explain anything to. And without that constant pressure… something inside me *moved*.

Not a thought.

Not a choice.

A *compulsion*.

I felt pulled — **compelled** — to buy **bras** and **dresses**. Not just to imagine them, or daydream about them. But to *own* them. To wear them. To feel them *against the skin that finally belonged to me*.

And when the bras arrived in the mail?

I slipped one on — and **what do you know**.

My B-sized breasts fit perfectly.

Not too much room.

Not too little.

Almost like…

Almost like they had always been there.

Like I had always been *her*.

And now she was done hiding.

But the world outside my bedroom door didn't match what was happening inside me.

Because unfortunately… I lived in the **ghetto**.

And as much as she — the *real me* — was starting to come forward…

She wasn't safe there.

So I did what I had always done.

I put her back in the closet.

Literally.

The bras. The dresses. The softness I had finally let myself feel — folded neatly and hidden behind other clothes. Out of sight. Not because I was ashamed… but because I didn't want to die.

I had taken vocational classes *back in high school* — in this very city. Now I had moved here, into the same streets where those classes once took place.

But this wasn't school anymore.
This was the **real world** version of it — and it wasn't friendly.

This city didn't pull punches.
It didn't care about softness, or truth, or femininity blooming in private bedrooms.

It was the kind of place where you had to watch your back — literally.

We weren't dealing with teenagers anymore.
We were dealing with **adults** — ones who would **stab you without a second thought** if they didn't like the way you looked, walked, or spoke.

So even though I had my own house now…
Even though she — the woman inside me — was starting to come forward…

I had to hide her again.

The bras. The dresses. The gentle pieces of who I was becoming — all folded and placed back in the closet. Not out of shame. But out of survival.

The city outside my window wasn't ready for her.
So for a little while longer… she would have to wait.

I stayed in that house for years.

It wasn't just shelter anymore.
It became a place of **healing**.

The kind of healing that doesn't happen overnight — the kind that's slow, uneven, honest. The kind that comes from forming **memories** instead of surviving moments.

In that house, I found myself again — not all at once, but in pieces.

I got off the **opiates**.

After so many years of being prescribed them — of relying on them just to make it through the day — they had started turning on me. I could feel it.

My **short-term memory** was slipping.

Moments blurred. Conversations vanished.

Pain relief came with a fog that was beginning to **erase me**.

So I made a choice.

I quit — and I did it fast.

I switched to a **natural pain reliever** — one you grow.

It wasn't about getting high.

It was about **getting clear**.

About staying present. About staying *me*.

And it worked.

I got my mind back.

I got my body back.

And slowly, I started feeling like a person again —
not a patient. Not a case file. Not a question mark in
a system that never understood me.

Just me.

Alive. A little bruised. But **home**.

But over time… things started to come to a
head.

The city I had once seen as a chance to rebuild
— the same streets where I made peace with my
past — **started to degrade**.

The neighborhood changed.

The cracks weren't in my foundation — they
were **all around it**.

The apartment next to mine brought in new
tenants.
At first, it was just noise.
Then it was traffic.
Then it was drugs.

I saw it happening. Watched the patterns.
And then came the worst part:

Their **customers** started driving by — slowly,
deliberately — and **pointing guns at me**.

Over and over.

No words. Just a silent threat.

They didn't care who I was.
Didn't care what I'd survived.
Didn't care that the woman they were targeting had
fought through grief, addiction, gender, and every
kind of erasure just to be here.

They saw me. And they saw a target.

And that's when I knew:

It was time to go.

So I listed my house.

The market was hot.

And for once, that worked in my favor.

We found a buyer — fast.

There was no drawn-out process, no endless showings, no months of waiting.

It felt like the universe, after everything, was finally clearing a path.

It wasn't just about selling a house.
It was about **leaving the danger behind**.
About protecting myself.
About protecting **Fenway**, who still stood guard by the door every night, loyal as ever.

The foundation I had poured — brick by brick, day by day — had done its job.

It held me up when I needed it most.
It gave me space to heal.
And now… it was time to build again.

Somewhere safer.

Somewhere quieter.

Somewhere **new**.

I was really hoping **Fenway** would make it with us.

We had found a new home — a peaceful little place in **rural Maine**, surrounded by quiet roads and fresh air. It was everything I had wanted. Everything *he* had deserved.

But the years hadn't been kind to him.

He was older now.

Slower.

Gentler than ever.

And hurting.

He had a **tumor on his leg**.

A **heart condition** the vets couldn't do much about. And every night I looked into his eyes, I could see him trying to hold on — for me.

We made the call two weeks before the closing.

The hardest call.

We let him go.

Not in pain. Not alone.
But with love. With dignity.
With every ounce of peace Lisa would've wanted for him.

He didn't make it to the new house.

But **he carried me to its door**.

And I will carry him — always.

As the home-visiting vet pulled out of my driveway, the sky opened up and it started to pour.
Was it just the weather?
Or was it Lisa — crying for Fenway?

Her hero. Her protector.

The last living piece of the life we shared.

As I drive over the border into Maine, everything I own packed tight in the car, something inside me exhales.

She exhales.

Not in words. Not in sound. But in presence — like a long-held breath finally released. She knows this is a safe place. Not perfect. Not painless. But safe enough to begin again. Safe enough to stop hiding in shadows and start stepping into the light.

For years, she lived behind my eyes. In secret glances. In soft moments I never let last too long. But now… she rides in the front seat. Watching the trees blur past. Feeling the quiet hum of possibility.

She's still cautious.

She knows the world outside doesn't always understand. That timing still matters. That truth, even when it's beautiful, can still be dangerous. But for the first time… she doesn't have to disappear.

Not here. Not anymore.

My father and stepmother planned a visit not long after I arrived. They brought my brother and nephews — all of them curious to see my new place, the house I had bought with pain-earned money and Lisa's legacy.

I was nervous.

Not because I didn't want them there… but because I knew she was close. Closer than she had ever been. Just beneath the surface, waiting.

They pulled into the driveway, wide eyes taking in the land — ten acres of peace, trees like sentries, the quiet kind of quiet you can only find in the middle of nowhere. Deer grazed lazily in the side yard, not even flinching as we stepped outside. It was a fortress of solitude. And for the first time in my life, the fortress was mine.

We shared meals. Laughed. Played games with the kids. My father admired the property, proud in the way men are when they see hard work turn into something physical, something real. No one knew what I was holding inside. No one saw the closet — not the one with the doors, but the one I had carried for decades.

After they left, I stood at the window and watched the woods breathe.

And I planned to set her free.

Not in rebellion. Not in spectacle. But in stillness. She had waited long enough.

After their last day visiting, I closed the door behind them.

And she burst through it.

There was no hesitation. No fear. No more asking for permission.

She didn't ease into the world — she claimed it.

The second the house was quiet, she took to the internet like a woman starved. Window shopping wasn't enough anymore. This wasn't about dreams. This was about decisions.

She picked out dresses — soft fabrics, flowing cuts, colors that made her feel alive. Skirts that danced in her imagination. Bras — real ones — no more hiding, no more wondering. Just hers.

She moved with urgency, like the years of waiting had finally caught up to her and now time was something to devour.

There was no longer a question of if she was real. She was. And she had a debit card.

A week later, her orders arrived.

Box after box — like care packages from the version of me that had been waiting her whole life to finally live.

She didn't waste a second.

I gathered all my old clothes — the ones that no longer felt like mine, no longer felt like truth. They didn't just feel wrong... they felt like lies. Camouflage. Costumes from a life I had been forced to perform.

I didn't burn them. I didn't need to. I just folded them, tucked them away, and locked the closet door. That part of my life was over.

She filled the dresser drawers with everything she had chosen. Cotton tanks. Soft panties. Bralettes. A skirt that made her feel light. A dress that whispered, you made it.

And as I slid the final drawer closed, something clicked inside me.

This wasn't pretend.

This wasn't dress-up.

This was mine now.

No more waiting.

She wasn't a secret anymore.

She was home.

Then came the moment.

Not a dramatic reveal. Not a movie scene. Just me, alone in my room, standing in front of a mirror.

But this time, I didn't see confusion.

I didn't see shame.

I didn't see a mask.

I saw her.

And for the first time, she saw me.

She wasn't some dream anymore. She wasn't locked inside or hidden beneath layers of fear.

She was real. Present. Complete.

This moment — this breath — was where everything aligned.

She knew her name.

And I knew mine.

She and I were one.

I am Ashley.

Now that I was in a new town, I had to start over with everything — including finding a new doctor. It took a while to get seen. Appointments were booked months out, and I wasn't sure how I'd be received. But eventually, I got in.

I remember that first visit like a snapshot.

The office was warm, quiet. No raised eyebrows when I signed in. No confusion over my name. They accepted me as Ashley — no questions, no hesitation. Just… acceptance.

When the nursing assistant brought me in, she smiled and said,

"I love your outfit. The color coordination is perfect."

And it wasn't just small talk.

It was affirmation.

It was a stranger seeing me, really seeing me, and responding with kindness — not judgment, not confusion, but kindness.

For so many years, I had walked into medical buildings and felt like an imposter. A question mark. A mistake on the paperwork.

But that day, I felt like a woman.

I felt like a person who belonged.

As my new doctor, Vanessa, entered the room, she smiled kindly and introduced herself.

Neither of us knew it at the time, but we were about to solve a fifteen-year mystery — one that had haunted my body, my identity, and every unanswered scan and symptom I had lived through.

I didn't feel comfortable diving into my old medical history. There was too much pain there. Too many moments of being dismissed, misdiagnosed, or ignored. I had signed the release forms, assuming everything would be transferred and shared.

But Vanessa never brought it up.

She never rattled off old test results. Never quoted back the words of doctors who got it wrong. She looked at me — not my file. And she listened to what I had to say now, in this moment.

And I felt something I hadn't felt in a long time. Relief.

Not because she had all the answers yet. But because, for once, the past wasn't being used against me.

The slate didn't just feel clean — it was.

My previous provider had never sent my records. Despite the release form I signed, nothing had been transferred. Vanessa didn't have pages of old charts or misdiagnoses to sift through. She had me — just me — sitting in front of her, ready to move forward. The air felt open.

And for the first time, I didn't feel like I had to explain my existence.

I got down to business.

I didn't tell Vanessa what I believed — that I thought my body was producing estrogen on its own, that I had suspicions about ovaries or even a uterus. I didn't dare say those words out loud.

Not because they weren't true.

But because I was afraid.

Afraid of what this state might do with that kind of information. Afraid of being labeled, dismissed — or worse.

This place still allows electroconvulsive therapy. Still calls it "treatment." Still trusts people with power to decide who is sane, who is real, and who needs to be fixed.

So I stayed quiet.

I didn't walk in with theories or truths too heavy for the system to carry.

Instead, I asked for a referral — just a referral to a gender clinic. A simple request. One that would trigger the tests I needed without raising red flags.

I played it safe.

But inside, I was burning with a truth I had never dared put into words before.

I needed answers.

And this was the only way to get them without risking everything.

It worked.

I got the referral.

To be honest, I wasn't surprised.

I was a wolf — not the kind that growls or bares teeth, but one that had honed her instincts over decades. I knew how to move through the system without raising alarms. I knew how to ask just enough, say just enough, be just enough to get what I needed without setting off the fear that kept so many others trapped.

This wasn't luck.

This was strategy. This was survival.

And I had sharpened those skills one painful year at a time.

While I waited for the appointment at the gender clinic, something unexpected happened.

I started living.

Real living — the kind where you do ordinary things, but they feel extraordinary because you're finally doing them as yourself.

I went food shopping every week, just like anyone else. But now I wasn't hiding in plain sight. I wasn't scanning the aisles in fear, afraid someone might see something "off." I was walking through those aisles as her — calm, soft, real.

And something shifted.

The women I passed didn't stare. They didn't scoff. They gave me nods. Smiles. Quiet looks of approval. The kind of silent acknowledgment women give each other in public — a language of sisterhood spoken with the eyes.

This wasn't just a home I had moved to.

It was a community.

One that didn't demand explanations. One that didn't ask me to prove I belonged.

They just let me be.

And for the first time in my life… I did.

Months passed.

No call back from the gender clinic.

I wasn't shocked — they were overwhelmed, buried in waitlists, and the recent election had only added fuel to the fire. More fear. More need. More people trying to find safe harbor in a world that kept moving the goalposts.

But I wasn't going to let silence stall me.
I had a yearly wellness visit scheduled with Vanessa
— just a routine checkup. Nothing special. But I
figured… maybe it was time to give things a little
nudge.
I had waited long enough.
So when she walked in, I smiled, sat up straight,
and decided: this time, we talk.
I didn't lay everything out. I wasn't ready for that.
Instead, I told her a white lie — not to deceive, but
to survive.
I said I was having hot flashes.
And technically… I wasn't lying. I had experienced
them — as a teenager, long before I had the
language for what they meant. But I let her think
they were happening now.
Just enough to raise a flag.
Just enough to warrant testing.
Just enough to nudge open the door I needed.
She didn't question it. Didn't doubt me. She just
nodded and said,
"Okay, I'm going to order a testosterone test."
Before I could stop myself, I blurted out—
"And an estrogen test too."
It came out fast. Too fast. The kind of truth that
slips past your fear and lands in the room before
you can reel it back in.
She raised an eyebrow.
There was a pause — not judgmental, just curious.

Then she said,
"Well… since we referred you to the gender clinic, I guess it couldn't hurt."
And just like that, the order was in.
That was all I needed.
The truth was finally on its way.
And this time, it would be written in blood.
I had to wait a few days for the estrogen test to come back.
I'll never forget the date: December 24th, 2024.
Christmas Eve.
It felt like the universe had finally wrapped up the truth and handed it to me — a quiet, sacred gift. Not under a tree, but in my patient portal.
I opened the results with shaking hands.
And there it was.
Estrogen total: 285 pg/mL.
A biological female level.
I stared at the number — not in shock, but in quiet validation.
This wasn't new. My body had been telling this story for years. Through the cycles. Through the pain. Through the confusion.
But now it was in writing.
Now it was real.
Now the world could finally see what I had always felt.
It was the first Christmas gift I ever received that truly felt like mine.
And then… came the wait.

The testosterone test was still processing.
One final number left to confirm everything I already knew in my bones.
The moment I saw the estrogen results, I didn't hesitate.
I downloaded a period tracker.
Not as a joke. Not as a game. But because it finally made sense.
My symptoms weren't random. My pain wasn't imagined. The timing — the waves of emotion, the physical shifts, the monthly pull in my lower abdomen — all of it pointed to something bigger.
So I gave it a name.
Cycle Day 1.
I didn't need a uterus on an ultrasound to know what my body was doing.
It was following a rhythm — a feminine rhythm.
And I was done pretending not to notice.
For the first time in my life, I wasn't asking permission to understand myself.
I was tracking her.
Me.
About a week later, the testosterone results came in.
429 ng/dL.
Low end of the male range — technically "normal," but only by a chart that never accounted for someone like me.
But I didn't need a medical journal to interpret it.
I already knew.
That number didn't cancel out the truth.

It confirmed it.

My estrogen was in the biological female range. My symptoms followed a clear 29-day cycle. And now my testosterone — hovering low — only made it more clear:

I was not a biological male.

I was intersex.

And I was trans.

This wasn't an identity I claimed out of rebellion or belief.

It was a body I had lived in.

A truth I had tracked in silence.

And now it had a name.

I wasn't confused.

I was complete.

A few days later, I logged into the patient portal and left a message for Vanessa.

I told her everything — the pain I had been living with for years, the CT scans that always came back "normal," the way doctors had shrugged it off like I was imagining it. I laid it all out.

She responded quickly.

She wanted to order another CT scan.

My heart sank.

I didn't want another scan that showed nothing. I wanted an ultrasound — something more focused, more deliberate, something that might actually see what everyone else kept missing.

So I scheduled an office visit.

When I sat down with Vanessa, I told her the truth.

"I've had eight or more CT scans over the years. They've never shown anything. Just empty reports. Cold language. No answers."
She listened.
Really listened.
Then she looked me in the eye and said something I wasn't expecting:
"This time will be different."
There was something in her voice — not pity, not protocol. Promise.
And for the first time in a very long time… I believed her.
So I agreed.
One more scan.
Not because I trusted the machine.
But because, maybe for once, I could trust the person ordering it.
I went for the CT scan a few days later.
I didn't expect much. I told myself not to get my hopes up — not after so many dead ends, so many "normal" results that never matched what I was living through.
But Vanessa was true to her word.
They found something.
Bilateral adrenal nodules.
I opened the scan report on my phone, right there in my living room — and everything inside me lit up.
Not with fear.
With rage.

The kind of rage that burns hotter than thermite —
fast, fierce, and unforgiving.
Fifteen years of pain. Fifteen years of dismissal.
Fifteen years of doctors telling me "there's nothing
wrong," "it's just in your head," "maybe it's stress."
And all I could hear echoing in my mind was:
"Them bastards. They lied to me."
They told me I was imagining it.
They told me my body didn't know what it was
saying.
They looked me in the eyes and called it mystery —
when the truth had been there all along.
I wasn't crazy.
I wasn't confused.
I wasn't weak.
I was right.

A switch flipped in my head.
It wasn't just about me anymore.
A new president had taken office — one already
targeting people like me. People born this way.
People who dared to live their truth out loud. The
attacks weren't subtle. They weren't accidental.
They were intentional — calculated attempts to
erase, legislate, and shame us back into silence.
And for the first time in my life, I stopped thinking
about just myself.
That fire — the one that had been burning since I
opened that scan report — it shifted.

It wasn't just rage anymore.
It was fuel.
I had spent so many years trying to survive. To stay
small. To stay quiet. To protect myself.
But now?
I was done hiding.
They tried to erase me.
Now I would use my voice to defend everyone they
said didn't deserve to exist.
I would speak for the ones still waiting for answers,
still trapped in closets built by silence and shame.
I had been ignored, mislabeled, misunderstood —
but not anymore.
They gave me fire.
And I was going to use it.
The period tracker I downloaded kept doing its
thing — logging symptoms, timing patterns,
tracking moods.
And after a few months… it was undeniable.
A 29-day cycle.
Like clockwork.
Cramping. Mood shifts. GI changes. Energy swings.
Emotional surges that peaked mid-cycle, like an
ovulation wave rolling through a body no one
believed could have one.
The tracker didn't lie.
Neither did my body.
When I showed the data to the specialists, their
faces said it all.
They were baffled.

They didn't have answers — not yet — just questions. A lot of them. And now I was being scheduled for more tests. Bloodwork. Imaging. Endocrine consults. The works.

But this time, it didn't feel like I was being doubted. It felt like I was being studied — not as a patient to fix, but as a person whose truth didn't fit the box.

They were finally listening.

And as much as part of me wanted answers, the truth is… I already had the one that mattered most.

My body wasn't broken.

It had just been ignored.

Some princesses are crowned not by magic, but by truth.

This is not the end of my story — it's just the beginning.

I don't need Disney to tell me I'm a princess.

My body knew this the whole time.

Acknowledgments

To Vanessa —
Thank you for seeing me when the world didn't.
For listening to my pain, believing what I felt, and helping me trust my body again.
You didn't just treat symptoms — you helped me reclaim myself. I will always be grateful.

To Eve and Alyssa —
Your voices on *Chewed Gum* found me in one of the darkest chapters of my life.
You didn't know it, but you gave me the focus and clarity I needed to survive — and to finish this book.
You helped turn chaos into purpose. You helped me remember who I was.

To everyone who reads this —
Thank you for holding space for my story.
Thank you for sitting with the raw, the painful, the beautiful, and the unfinished.
If something in these pages helped you feel seen, you are the reason I wrote it.

This is more than a book. It's a spark.
And if it lit something in you, let it burn.

With love,
Ashley J. Webb